MESO
KILLERS

A SAGA OF
CORPORATE GREED, LIES,
AND THE
Painful Deaths of American Workers

JOSEPH P. SHANNON

Shannon Law Group
A Professional Corporation

Shannon Law Group, P.C.

Chicago Office
135 S. LaSalle, Suite 2200
Chicago, Illinois 60603

Woodridge Office
3550 Hobson Road, Suite 403
Woodridge, Illinois 60517

www.shannonlawgroup.com

Tel: 312.578.9501
Fax: 312.268.5474
Email: joseph@shannonlawgroup.com

Printed in the United States of America.

ISBN: 978-1-63385-352-2

Designed and published by

Word Association Publishers
205 Fifth Avenue
Tarentum, Pennsylvania 15084

www.wordassociation.com
1.800.827.7903

DISCLAIMER

This book is informative in nature. It does not constitute as legal advice.

If you need legal advice, please follow the advice in this book to find and retain an attorney. Only an attorney fully apprised of the particular facts of your situation can provide the legal advice you need.

The law applicable to mesothelioma cases varies from state to state. Where the information in this book is Illinois-specific, I point that out. Otherwise, this advice is generally applicable throughout the United States.

Included in this book are some examples and stories from actual cases I tried or on which I worked. To protect the privacy of those involved, the names and identifying details have been changed.

CONTENTS

FOREWORD

Mesothelioma strikes without discrimination. But, given the history of asbestos in our society, it hit the Greatest Generation the hardest.

My dad retired at 62. He was looking forward to three things: golfing, traveling, and playing with his grandchildren. This was before he was diagnosed with mesothelioma.

After the bombing of Pearl Harbor, my dad dropped out of high school at age 17. He then joined the Navy and served a tour in World War II. During that time, asbestos was commonly used in naval vessels. As such, naval vessels and shipyards were probably the first places where my dad was exposed to asbestos products.

When he moved back home to Springfield, Illinois, he got a job as an electrician at the Pillsbury Mill plant. The plant was a major landing point for WWII vets. For 40 years, my dad worked the first shift, six days a week at the plant. I don't remember him uttering a single word of complaint during the entire four decades he was there. The plant was likely the second and more extensive place where my dad was exposed to asbestos containing products.

Between working six days a week and raising me and my four sisters, my dad didn't have much time for golf. That's why he started taking golf lessons at the Park District. He also fondly remembered his experience "traveling" (i.e., serving naval tours of duty in WWII) and wanted to share that with my mother in retirement. And, of course, he wanted more time to spend with his grandchildren.

My dad was 60 when he first started experiencing a discomfort or twitch in his chest. Doctors originally told him it was nothing serious. He tried to work through it until it was too painful to ignore. The pain was slowing him down from golfing, gardening, and working with his hands around the house. But the hardest part for him was when he grew weaker. My dad was so weak that he could no longer play with or carry his grandchildren. One by one, he lost the ability to do each of those as the pain progressed. After nearly a year of pain, he was finally diagnosed with mesothelioma.

My dad spent his two years of retirement battling a horrendous cancer. He never got to golf or travel in retirement. He did live to see two of his five daughters married, and he got to meet, and dearly loved, three of his grandchildren. He passed away at 65.

As hard as it was for my dad, I think those years were even harder for his family. His children were front and center in his last days. My sisters and other dedicated relatives and friends (he had so many people who cared for him) made sure he was never alone, organizing and taking him to all his appointments and treatments. It was a burden my mom couldn't bear to see, and she struggled to continue parenting her daughters and working part-time.

My mom is in her nineties and is living his lost future alone. She has now seen three of her daughters' weddings and the births of their grandchildren without him. Most of all, my parents never got to travel the world together as they had dreamed.

The average age that a person is diagnosed with mesothelioma is 69. It's ironic that the great majority of those who contract, suffer, and die from mesothelioma develop it from asbestos exposure at work—but it is diagnosed just in time for retirement. That is what happened to my dad; he spent a lifetime saving and doing the right thing just to die when he was about to enjoy the rewards of his labor. My dad never would have complained about that, but it was hard for his family.

My dad would never have said anything bad about the plant or the Navy. He wasn't built that way. The plant eventually closed in 2001, years after his retirement. Asbestos cleanup over its massive 18-acre property isn't completed, even to this day.

All over America, there were companies that knew about the dangers of asbestos exposure and consciously concealed this danger from their workers, all while those workers were unknowingly exposed to asbestos that can lead to a horrible and excruciating death. These companies profited on the labor of those they exposed to these dangerous products.

If only their morals were as developed as my dad's.

-Kate Refine

Kate Refine is the daughter of Harry Refine. She is a former team member of Shannon Law Group, P.C. Kate and her husband Tim have three children, Madeline, Henry, and Will. Kate and Tim live in Naperville, Illinois.

CHAPTER 1:
MESOTHELIOMA & THE MINERAL OF DEATH

WHAT IS MESOTHELIOMA?

Mesothelioma is a form of cancer of the tissue that lines organs, particularly of the lungs and chest wall. The great majority of mesothelioma diagnoses are caused by exposure to asbestos. While asbestos can cause a number of health problems, mesothelioma is often the most fatal.

Individuals who develop mesothelioma were most likely exposed to asbestos at work or lived with someone who brought asbestos fibers home from work on their clothes and equipment.

By some estimates, 3,000 new cases of mesothelioma are diagnosed annually in the United States. These numbers are actually increasing despite diminished use of asbestos in the U.S. Symptoms of mesothelioma include shortness of breath, swollen abdomen, chest wall pain, cough, exhaustion, and weight loss. Due to the disease's long latency period, it can take between 15 and 50 or more years after the first instance of asbestos exposure for mesothelioma symptoms to appear.

WHAT IS ASBESTOS?

Asbestos is a naturally occurring bundle of mineral fibers found in rocks and soil. It used to be called a "miracle mineral" because it is very resistant to heat, electricity, and chemicals. Because of these properties, it was widely used in construction materials, automotive parts, and fire resistant textiles for decades.

Today, however, it is well understood that asbestos is a toxic and carcinogenic pathogen: the mineral of death. In fact, asbestos remains the number one cause of occupational cancer in the United States, and it accounts for 54 percent of all occupational cancers.

Asbestos fibers can separate very easily into tiny pieces when handled or damaged. When inhaled or swallowed, these fibers can build up in the chest or abdominal cavity, where they scar and damage the tissue over time. Over several decades, this continual scarring can eventually lead to mesothelioma.

When asbestos is encountered in large quantities or is disturbed and distributed into the air (such as when a building is demolished or a home is remodeled), it becomes a health risk. Loose asbestos fibers are odorless and tasteless. What's more, asbestos that is manufactured into products or building materials cannot be detected by visual examination—it must be detected through laboratory testing.

There is no safe level of asbestos exposure. The longer and more frequent the exposure, the more likely an individual is to develop asbestos-related disease like mesothelioma.

Asbestos that is manufactured into products or building materials **cannot be detected by visual examination—** it must be detected through laboratory testing.

CHAPTER 2:
ANCIENT ASBESTOS

When thinking of asbestos, one may recall the horrendous asbestos-related injuries suffered by millions of Americans, the cover ups by asbestos manufacturers, or the massive class action lawsuits that followed.

What many people don't know is that humans have been using asbestos for millennia.

Ancient Greek, Egyptian, Chinese, and Roman civilizations used asbestos in pottery, embalming rituals, wicks, fireproof linens and clothing, burial shrouds, lamps, weapons, paper, and a myriad of other uses. Asbestos has even been found in Stone Age pottery predating recorded history. Simply put, people have been using asbestos since the dawn of civilization.

For these ancient civilizations, asbestos was like magic. Ancient Egyptians used asbestos for the wicks in the burial tombs of pharaohs. Romans made table linen from asbestos and cleaned it by throwing it into a fire.

Asbestos has been relevant to society for a long time. But it wasn't nearly as commonly used in ancient civilizations as it was during the Industrial Revolution and Twentieth Century.

Despite this, it was known even in ancient times that asbestos was a hazard.

Greek and Roman historians documented how asbestos caused a "sickness of the lungs." Roman slaves who mined or worked with asbestos would fashion makeshift respirators from animal bladders to limit asbestos inhalation.

However, asbestos was rare, and the ability of historians to share knowledge was limited, so this wisdom was not passed down in time to save millions of lives that asbestos-related diseases, such as mesothelioma, would later claim.

It was known **even in ancient times** that asbestos was a hazard.

CHAPTER 3:

THE RISE OF BIG ASBESTOS: THE INDUSTRIAL REVOLUTION

Ancient and medieval uses of asbestos were often a novelty. Asbestos manufacturing truly boomed into a major industry in the late 1800s at the start of the Industrial Revolution.

Asbestos use in building materials traces as far back as 1858. That year, the H.W. Johns Manufacturing Company (predecessor to the infamous Johns Manville Company) began selling fireproof roofing materials using asbestos.

The demand for asbestos took off in the late 1800s; it was used in both building materials in factories and in many commercial products. New inventions harnessing the power of steam and electricity required a strong and cost effective material resistant to fire, heat, electricity, and chemicals. Asbestos fit this demand perfectly.

The U.S. quickly became the world's greatest consumer of asbestos. It would hold this dubious distinction for the better part of a century.

The railroad industry was the first to use asbestos and asbestos-containing products extensively. The shipyard industry wasn't far behind, followed by the automobile industry. All of these industries needed fireproof parts—and, in the case of ships, fireproof vessels. Some of the products and places today still contain asbestos.

Workers in these industries were hit the hardest by asbestos-related diseases decades later. The shipbuilding industry was especially dangerous in war time, as it peaked with millions of workers building and repairing ships.

The dangers of asbestos began appearing at the end of the 19th century. Even in the face of these early warnings, asbestos production only increased worldwide, with the U.S. being the primary consumer and destination of asbestos.

The U.S. quickly became the world's greatest consumer of asbestos. It would hold this dubious distinction for the better part of a century.

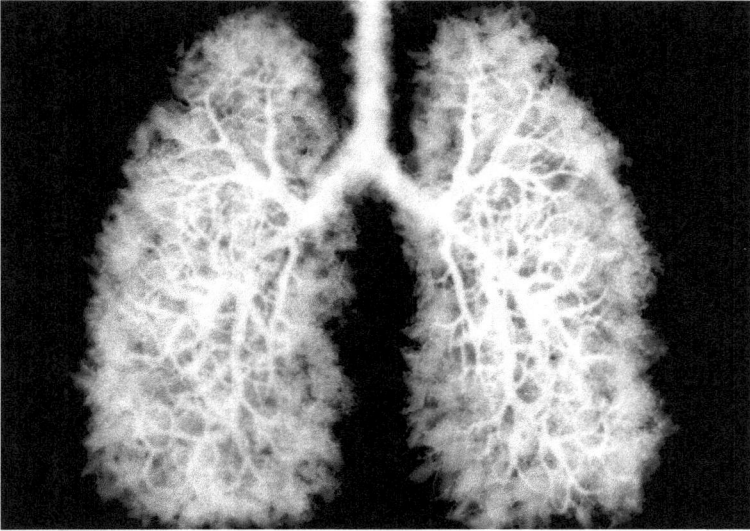

CHAPTER 4:

EARLY AWARENESS OF
THE DANGERS OF ASBESTOS

Even as asbestos was making inroads to every facet of American manufacturing, including homes, businesses, and vehicles across the country, doctors and researchers were already documenting the dangers of asbestos exposure.

In the late 1890s and early 1900s, several isolated cases of asbestos-related disease were documented. An Austrian doctor attributed one patient's pulmonary disease to asbestos exposure. A report on English factories noted that the "widespread damage and injury to the lungs [was] due to the dusty surrounding of the asbestos mill."

In 1906, Dr. Montague Murray at London's Charing Cross Hospital documented the first death of an asbestos worker from pulmonary failure. The autopsy revealed that the 33-year-old victim had large amounts of asbestos fibers in his lungs. Not long after, reports and studies of asbestos workers around the world began documenting that they were dying unnaturally young. By 1908, insurance companies began raising premiums and decreasing benefits for asbestos workers. Despite this, the actual mechanisms of disease were not yet well understood.

In 1924, an English doctor made the first diagnosis of asbestosis. The victim was a woman who had worked with asbestos since she was 13. She died at the age of 33.

In the 1930s, medical journals detailed results from clinical examinations of hundreds of asbestos workers and concluded that one in four workers was suffering from asbestosis. Some of these articles specifically proposed that workers should be warned in order to assure and understand the risk they encountered in continuing to work with asbestos. Articles also noted that many cases of asbestosis had likely been misdiagnosed as tuberculosis or other pulmonary diseases, and the extent of the asbestos epidemic was likely far greater than any had previously expected.

In the 1930s, journals also began publishing articles linking asbestos with cancer. However, in the 1940s, the link between cancer and asbestos was more thoroughly explored. In 1943, the first case of a mesothelioma-like tumor was reported in a German study. By 1947, it was reported that 13 percent of asbestosis cases were accompanied by cancer in the lungs or pleura. By 1949, the Journal of the American Medical Association concluded that asbestos was likely linked to occupational cancer. In 1955, epidemiological studies demonstrated that asbestos workers had a tenfold risk above the general population of contracting lung cancer. Studies in the 1960s would later confirm that the family members of asbestos workers also faced a greatly increased risk of cancer.

As a result of these early publications, a handful of sick employees filed lawsuits against the Johns-Manville company, which eventually settled their claims. This is discussed in more detail in Chapter 5.

Around this time, asbestos awareness was eclipsed in the public consciousness by alarm over another deadly industrial lung disease: silicosis. Silicosis was a scourge caused by rock dust. It greatly impacted miners for generations. This was a fateful development for asbestos litigation.

By 1949, the Journal of the American Medical Association concluded that asbestos was likely linked to occupational cancer.

CHAPTER 5:

EVADING RESPONSIBILITY: A CORPORATE COVER-UP

One would think that the major victories for workers with silica-related respiratory disease might have been a warning to employers to improve working conditions and find replacements for asbestos in their equipment, facilities, and products. On the contrary, they actually had the opposite effect. Manufacturers and employers whose workers were exposed to asbestos took this as an opportunity to hide the truth about asbestos from their workers.

Although medical journals were publishing articles about asbestos, public awareness of its dangers was not yet widespread enough to spur significant action to protect workers.

Asbestos companies continued using asbestos in manufacturing and construction with impunity. Even as safer alternatives were being developed, such as fiberglass insulation, many manufacturers simply ignored these costlier alternatives. They knowingly put their workers in danger for the sake of profit.

To say that asbestos manufacturers and users' levels of concern about their customers and employees were not urgent would be an understatement. One union of two of the most notorious industries in world history, tobacco and asbestos, were briefly and horrifically married to produce a "safer" cigarette.

In 1952, Readers Digest published a series of articles entitled "Cancer by the Carton," about the health risks of tobacco. Cigarette manufacturers looking to reassure the public and increase sales began adding filters to the cigarettes. One company in particular, Kent, went the extra mile to make a fire-resistant super filter, made with one of the deadliest forms of asbestos. Kent launched a hugely successful advertising campaign for its "micronite filter," touting it as an enhancement that protected smokers from harm.

At this point, medical studies had linked asbestos to respiratory disorders for over 50 years. After negative publicity, Kent commissioned studies to show that no asbestos fibers were released into smokers' lungs. Of course, the studies revealed the opposite—the filters released massive amounts of asbestos into users' lungs. Kent discontinued the filters in 1956, four years after introducing them.

In the 1940s, there might have been some abatement in asbestos based on the publications linking asbestos to respiratory disease. However, the demand for asbestos rocketed back up both during and after World War II as countries went to war and rebuilt after it. Asbestos usage continued to increase and hit its highest levels in the 1940s and 1970s, peaking with 804,000 tons consumed in the United States in 1973.

Even as asbestos production hit its highest levels, the asbestos industry had no appetite to take responsibility for its role in the disaster and no inclination to pay its victims fair compensation for their injuries. In fact, these companies did not even provide employees with protection against asbestos exposure.

One of the biggest asbestos manufacturers was the Johns-Manville Corporation. For decades, Johns-Manville hid evidence of the role of asbestos in disease from both the public and from its own ailing workers. Johns-Manville's management, like that of many asbestos manufacturers and sellers at the time, consciously decided to cover up the disease-causing nature of asbestos, knowing full well that hundreds of its own workers would die of diseases caused by their own products and workplace.

In 1949, Dr. Kenneth W. Smith, Corporate Medical Director for Johns-Manville, summarized Johns-Manville's corporate medical strategy in his memo to his corporate superiors:

> The fibrosis of this disease is irreversible and permanent so that eventually compensation will be paid to each of these men. But, as long as the man is not disabled it is felt that he should not be told of his condition so that he can live and work in peace and the company can benefit from his many years of experience.

Asbestos manufacturers knew of these dangers but denied them for years before they were eventually undeniable. In an internal 1988 memorandum, Johns-Manville representatives wrote that the company had falsely denied knowledge of the dangers of asbestos for decades, at least back to 1934. Johns-Manville had even sued its insurers and the U.S. government on theories based on the company's own feigned ignorance of the dangers of asbestos. An internal memo dated August 12, 1969 from Travelers, Manville's insurer, quoted one Manville attorney as saying "confidentially, Manville has been contaminating the 'Hell' out of both the air and the water for quite some time":

> In the Fatchko case it is felt we have no chance of winning when it is litigated since it is evident that Johns-Manville had contaminated both air and water in the past. In fact a Johns-Manville attorney stated, "Confidentially Johns-Manville has been contaminating the 'Hell' out of both the air and the water for quite some time." It is apparent Johns-Manville is concerned and frightened over the implications.

The documents, the report concluded, "demonstrate that Manville officers, directors, and employees . . . held secret information that had it been revealed, would have prevented the deaths of thousands of people." As part of the cover-up, Manville threatened that if the conspiracy became known, some of its employees would be indicted for manslaughter. Manville filed false tax documents concealing its known liability risks. Manville also unlawfully refused to produce documents demonstrating their knowledge of asbestos dangers when required in courts across the nation.

While Johns-Manville Corporation was the most visible perpetrator, it was far from unique in its role as a corporation hiding the effects of asbestos exposure from the public.

In a series of internal correspondence, the President of W.R. Grace Company instructed one manager who knew the dangers of asbestos to "stay unscrupulous, unethical, mean and selling Mono-Kote." A later letter clarified the game plan for covering up the dangers of their products, stating "the point I am trying to get across is that our present policy is to tell no one anything, no visitors, or discussion about our operations, period." Some years later, in response to a suggestion of an epidemiological study on the impact of asbestos for which the company might be responsible, a "personal and confidential" memo stated "I believe that the results of any study of this nature would become public knowledge within a relatively short period of time . . . I would advise against proceeding."

Attached to a Dow report on how the company was investigating asbestos was a hand written note not included in the report, noting "we are in trouble [and] would be more so if we had an investigation. We need a crash program."

In an internal 1988 memorandum, Johns-Manville representatives wrote that the company had falsely denied knowledge of the dangers of asbestos for decades, at least back to 1934.

CHAPTER 6:

THE FALL OF BIG ASBESTOS: WAVES OF LIABILITY

By the 1970s, asbestos exposure had grown to earn its common title as the worst occupational health disaster in U.S. history. By this time, asbestos manufacturers could no longer play dumb. The public was beginning to understand the dangers of asbestos. Workers were demanding safer and healthier working conditions, while liability claims against major asbestos manufacturers caused many of them to make and market asbestos substitutes.

The question remained, however, for the millions sickened by asbestos and the millions more who would become sick. How would they be compensated?

Although some of the landmark asbestos studies and publications were widely publicized by the 1960s, it wasn't until the 1970s that lawyers representing asbestos victims began scoring significant victories. Early asbestos cases were risky because they addressed issues on a scale that had never been addressed before. They also required the introduction of scientific evidence linking asbestos disease with their client's symptoms, as well as extensive factual investigation demonstrating a link between an individual asbestos producer and their client's asbestos exposure to show that a manufacturer or employer was a party responsible for the injury.

Those early defendants were large corporations who weren't afraid to fight dirty. They engaged in protracted litigation and fought at every turn. They challenged the asbestos victims frequently in their lawsuits, from whether the plaintiffs had actually been exposed to *their* asbestos (as opposed to asbestos from some other source) to technical issues like whether plaintiffs filed their lawsuits at the right time, in the right place.

Plaintiff attorneys who could not withstand years or decades of delay in payment or who could not advance thousands of dollars for investigation, scientific analysis, and testimony were forced out of the arena. Few plaintiff lawyers were willing to take asbestos workers' claims at that time, and those that did faced substantial risk.

In 1973, in the case of *Borel v. Fibreboard*, the Fifth Circuit Federal Court of Appeals found asbestos manufacturers strictly liable to workers as a result of exposure to their products. This decision established that defendants in the product supply chain may be jointly liable for latent injury torts.

In the early successful cases against asbestos manufacturers, plaintiff attorneys introduced evidence that major asbestos manufacturers had known of the dangers of asbestos as early as the 1930s, but had concealed that information from their employees and people exposed to asbestos-containing products. In 1978, a South Carolina judge issued a ruling finding that asbestos companies had undergone a "conscious effort" to suppress information on the dangers of asbestos exposure in order to avoid lawsuits.

In the following years, plaintiff lawyers successfully challenged other limitations to recovery for their clients, such as workers' compensation exclusivity. This freed injured employees to seek damages in tort.

By the mid-1980s, it was clear that asbestos victims could succeed against asbestos defendants by filing large numbers of claims, grouping them together, and negotiating with defendants on behalf of the entire group. Defendants would agree to settle the big groups of claims to cut down on their litigation costs. While this method may have cost some plaintiffs with strong cases some of their potential damages, it allowed plaintiff lawyers to settle weaker claims that would be hard to resolve alone. This, in turn, reduced the risk of representing asbestos claimants.

Following the *Borel* decision, product liability claims against asbestos manufacturers flooded into the courts. By the early 1980s, more than 20,000 claimants had filed lawsuits alleging exposure from asbestos.

The Johns-Manville Corporation filed for bankruptcy in 1982. It was the largest company ever to file for bankruptcy at the time, and it was 181st on the Fortune 500. It buckled under the weight of 16,500 asbestos lawsuits targeting it at that time alone. Many other asbestos companies followed.

In 1978, a South Carolina judge issued a ruling finding that asbestos companies had undergone a "conscious effort" to suppress information on the dangers of asbestos exposure in order to avoid lawsuits.

CHAPTER 7:
ASBESTOS ABATEMENT

Asbestos mining in the U.S. peaked in 1973 with a record of 137,000 metric tons mined. That same year, 803,000 metric tons were consumed in the U.S. alone. By 2009, asbestos consumption declined to only 900 tons per year.

In 2002, the last U.S. asbestos mine closed in California. Despite these closures, some mines with particularly deadly varieties of asbestos are still major public hazards. In Libby, Montana, a closed mine once operated by W.R. Grace Company continues to be one of the worst man-made environmental disasters, causing thousands of illnesses and deaths. In 2009, it was declared a public health emergency by the EPA.

Asbestos has been fully and partially banned in developed countries throughout the world, including the entire European Union. Asbestos use in the U.S. is not currently banned *per se*, but it is heavily regulated. Many uses of asbestos are forbidden by the Toxic Substances Control Act of 1989. It can only be used today in products that have historically used asbestos and only if there is no adequate substitute. This means it is typically used in protective clothing, cement, brake linings, and for other applications that require its fireproof properties. In addition, the regulation continues to ban "new uses" of asbestos, or uses that were not common historically.

In truth, it was likely massive liability in the courtroom—even more so than environmental and health regulations—that ultimately forced a decline to the use of asbestos. Still, the clean up was (and remains) a monumental task. Even today, 12,000 to 15,000 people die each year from asbestos-related diseases in the U.S. alone. At conservative estimates, that's 1 out of every 125 American men who die over the age of 50.

Asbestos has been fully and partially banned in developed countries throughout the world, including the entire European Union. Asbestos use in the U.S. is not currently banned *per se*, but it is heavily regulated.

Further, while it can be found in some products, much of asbestos contaminates the environment because it was poorly contained. For decades, asbestos was handled haphazardly. Since many were unaware of its toxicity, millions of workers would handle or come into contact with it on a daily basis without taking any precautions, including using safety gear.

Also, household asbestos exposure still presents some risk. Houses built prior to 1980 may have asbestos components, including insulation, cement, drywall, ceiling tiles, floor tiles, and other construction items. While intact, these items typically don't present a risk, but there is always potential for them to release asbestos into the air if damaged.

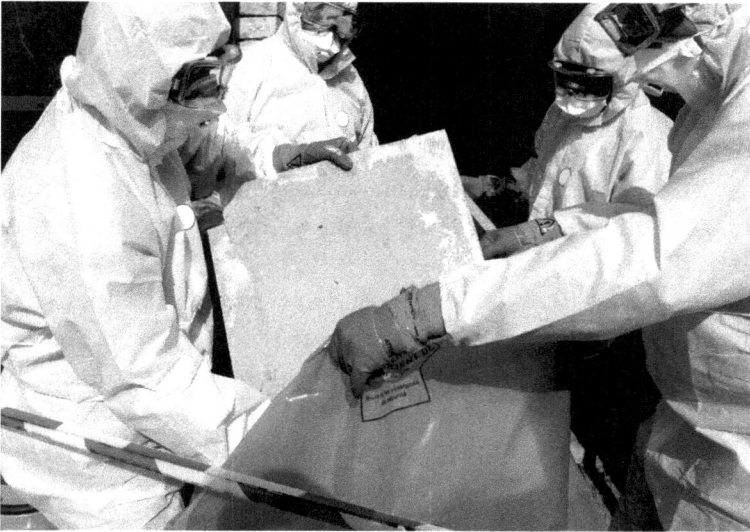

CHAPTER 8:

ASBESTOS LITIGATION IN THE UNITED STATES

Asbestos litigation is the largest and single most impactful mass tort litigation in the history of the U.S. justice system.

Medical science took time to identify asbestos as the cause of the malignant ailments afflicting tens of thousands of workers. Likewise, the legal system took time to recognize the rights of those workers to compensation for their injuries. As a result, a tidal wave of litigation was unleashed when those claims were finally recognized as valid. This tidal wave toppled many of the worst offenders in the asbestos trade.

In 1973, asbestos manufacturers were found strictly liable to workers injured as a result of exposure to their products (*Borel v. Fibreboard*, Fifth Circuit U.S. Court of Appeals, 1973). Following that decision, increasing numbers of product liability claims against asbestos manufacturers flowed into the courts.

In the 1980s, over 20,000 claimants had initiated lawsuits for asbestos injuries, and that number is only growing.

Asbestos litigation is the longest-running mass tort litigation in U.S. history, and it has shaped the way mass tort litigation works in this country for several reasons.

First, asbestos cases are an unusual fit in the traditional tort system, which is designed to address traumatic injuries that arise from a single occurrence (e.g., car crashes, slip-and-fall incidents, injuries from defective products, etc.).

In comparison, when an individual is injured in a car crash, it is immediately apparent who is involved, who may be at fault, who was injured, and the extent of their injuries. In contrast, most individuals exposed to asbestos do not develop any symptoms at all, even if they may experience some physiological indicators of disorder. Where symptoms do appear, they may vary greatly in intensity—individuals suffering from mesothelioma face a graver diagnosis than those with thickening of the lungs, for example.

When symptoms do develop, they usually appear 20 to 40 years after exposure. Therefore, it can be hard to determine who is responsible for the exposure, especially since a person can come into contact with hundreds of asbestos sources during their lifetime.

The sheer scope of the harm done, in combination with the uncertainty surrounding symptoms related to asbestos diseases, has created issues around litigating asbestos claims.

One major concern is the question of how to fairly divide compensation among claimants. The scope of harm caused by asbestos is enormous. The full extent of its damages is unknown and will not be known for years to come. Moreover, the resources available to compensate asbestos victims are limited.

Related to this concern is how to divide the fault among different defendants regarding degree of responsibility. An individual may come in contact with dozens of asbestos sources during their lifetime. And those sources, whether they are building materials, equipment, products, or environmental hazards, may each have had many suppliers, manufacturers, operators, owners or other parties who are responsible for causing the exposure. How is fault to be attributed among them?

Another concern about mesothelioma compensation is when victims should take legal action. In typical torts, individuals are expected to act as soon as possible to preserve their rights. States create statutes of limitations as deadlines by which people have to file their lawsuit, because waiting two, three, four, or more years can let evidence go stale and make claims harder to resolve. These statutes are typically between one and five years for personal injuries.

However, with asbestos exposure, individuals typically don't experience any symptoms for 20 to 40 years. Furthermore, they may learn of some minor symptom but not know that a serious disease may develop in the future. States are now confronted with the question of when these victims should be required to file claims to preserve their rights.

This differs sharply from the norm with most mass torts. Typically, once the claimed injuries are understood, the parties negotiate a settlement that resolves all or most claims.

Asbestos litigation has proven remarkably resistant to any uniform means of resolution, or any one system or resolution at all.

Instead, not only have asbestos cases persisted, but the systems of resolution have changed over the decades. Judges who presided over early asbestos litigation and developed their own systems and methods have retired or moved on, leaving new generations of judges and resolution systems in their wake. Also, given the scope of the damages caused by asbestos, many culpable parties have declared bankruptcy. This has shifted much of the battle from traditional courtrooms to bankruptcy court. In addition, it has forced victims and their attorneys to cast wider nets, drawing in new culpable parties who played roles in the asbestos manufacturing supply chain.

As a result, individual states—and even counties—have developed their own rules and procedures to streamline and expedite the asbestos claim process.

Moreover, there are growing concerns on all sides that the cost of settling a large amount of claims filed in recent years will deplete funds needed to compensate claimants who will eventually become seriously ill. This is particularly pressing when there are many mass settlements in which several claimants are rapidly depleting the pool of resources available for compensation.

On the whole, asbestos lawsuits typically target manufacturers' failure to protect workers against exposure and failure to warn workers to take adequate precautions against exposure.

With asbestos exposure, individuals typically don't experience any symptoms for 20 to 40 years.

CHAPTER 9:

PROCEDURAL SOLUTIONS FOR VICTIMS' RECOVERY

The growing volume of asbestos litigation has long been the subject of attention from public policymakers. Many seek to streamline the process to reduce the burden on both courts and parties alike.

For decades, especially as memories of asbestos manufacturers' wrongdoings were fresh in the public's mind, the burden of asbestos litigation seemed manageable, and its aims appeared important enough to avoid procedural shortcuts putting efficiency above effective and fair adjudication of individual claims.

In recent years, the situation has changed with steep increases of annual claims filing and a broadening of the defendants being named in individual cases. Those increasing and broadening costs have spurred more defendants and their insurers to push for procedures and mechanisms.

The increased litigation volume has also challenged victims who are finding the smaller pool of funds left over by major asbestos companies to be insufficient to compensate them for their injuries. As a result, some plaintiff groups are seeking procedural mechanisms to reduce their litigation costs and to divide awards among remaining claimants.

The most significant developments in asbestos litigation have been:

(1) the failure of global class action settlements;
(2) the reemergence of deferred dockets as a popular court management tool;
(3) increased frequency and scale of consolidated trials; and
(4) the increased use of bankruptcy reorganization to develop administrative processes for resolving current and future claims.

Many courts, including ones in Illinois, have been overwhelmed with long queues of claimants who have not yet manifested a legally identifiable injury. By extension, these courts also face statute of limitation issues with these cases.

In response, they have developed formal and informal procedures to manage these cases, including deferred dockets, inactive dockets, or pleural registries. These systems allow unimpaired asbestos victims to address their claims as they wait for their injuries to develop to the point where they can support a legal claim. Typically, this means that nonmalignant claims must meet certain criteria to proceed to the next step.

Another procedural variation is an "expedited docket," which give priority to cancer claims, placing those claims above others without any functional impairment.

Trial consolidation offers an additional way to manage asbestos cases by expediting litigation. Trial consolidation includes informal group settlement, multidistrict litigation, state multidistrict rules, class actions, and consolidation.

Consolidation litigation has been controversial because it raises due process questions from both sides. Judges have expressed doubts about the appropriateness of mass consolidations. However, other judges in charge of asbestos dockets see it as the only efficient way to handle litigation of this scale.

If the liability phase is tried first and the jury decides for the defendant, all of the plaintiffs lose. Oftentimes, plaintiffs won't even have the opportunity to argue for themselves.

In some instances, judges have consolidated hundreds or thousands of claims for trial. But there is little case law on selecting representative parties for this litigation. Judges appear to select representatives on an *ad hoc* basis. This process involves determining one or several asbestos cases, then applying the results to multiple disputes in the consolidation. For instance, from 1993 to 2001, there were over a dozen large-scale consolidated trials of 100 asbestos claims or more.

In that same period, there were 526 jury trials that reached verdicts on 1,570 plaintiffs' claims. About 60 percent of these trials involved a single claim. Most consolidated trials involved fewer than ten claims. But only 25 percent of all claims were tried individually; about 50 percent were tried in groups of six or more. Moreover, the number of plaintiffs in these cases had little difference in outcomes.

In the mid-1980s, plaintiff law firms representing large groups of asbestos victims were successful against some shipyards and petrochemical defendants. They achieved this by filing large numbers of claims, grouping them together, and negotiating with defendants on behalf of the entire group as a whole. In response, defendants would often settle such grouped claims to reduce litigation costs and contain outlying risk of major awards on serious claims. For the plaintiff firms, this also significantly reduced litigation risk.

Trial consolidation offers an additional way to manage asbestos cases by expediting litigation. Trial consolidation includes informal group settlement, multidistrict litigation, state multidistrict rules, class actions, and consolidation.

CONCLUSION

If you have been injured by asbestos exposure, your financial recovery is of vital importance not only to yourself, but to your family. The first and most important step in that recovery is finding the right lawyer for you.

I wrote this book mindful of our clients reading it who may be going through a difficult time. I hope that the information here helps you understand not only why finding the right attorney is important, but how to find and evaluate an attorney that will fight successfully for you.

For individuals injured by the negligent acts and omissions of others, the effects can be devastating, but the law is on your side. With the right representation and an understanding of the process, the legal system can be an important tool to put your family economy back on its feet. I hope you succeed in finding the attorney who will help you do so.

I hope that the information here helps you understand not only why finding the right attorney is important, but how to find and evaluate an attorney that will fight successfully for you.

MESOTHELIOMA AND ASBESTOS CASES

Q: WHAT IS ASBESTOS?

Asbestos is a naturally occurring mineral fiber found in rocks and soil. It used to be called a "miracle mineral" because it is so resistant to heat, electricity and chemicals. It was used widely for years in construction materials, automotive parts, and fire-resistant textiles because of these properties.

Today, however, it is well understood that asbestos is a toxic and carcinogenic pathogen. In fact, asbestos remains the number one cause of occupational cancer in the United States and it accounts for 54 percent of all occupational cancers.

Asbestos fibers can separate very easily into tiny pieces when handled or damaged. These loose fibers, when inhaled or swallowed, build up in the respiratory system, which can cause diseases, such as asbestosis, lung cancer, and mesothelioma.

Asbestos becomes a health risk when it is encountered in large quantities or is disturbed and distributed into the air (such as when a building is demolished or a home remodeled). Loose asbestos fibers are odorless and tasteless, as well as invisible to the naked eye. They must be detected by laboratory testing.

There is no safe level of asbestos exposure. However, the longer and more intense the exposure, the more likely an individual is to develop an asbestos-related disease.

Q: IS ASBESTOS ILLEGAL IN THE UNITED STATES?

Today, asbestos is banned in more than 50 countries throughout the world—but not the U.S.. While not banned, asbestos use and removal is heavily regulated by the Environmental Protection Agency (EPA) and other government entities. Asbestos can now be used only in products that have historically used asbestos and only if there is no adequate substitute. It is typically used in products that require fireproof properties such as protective clothing, cement, and brake linings.

As a result, use of asbestos in new products and construction use has decreased steeply in the United States since its peak in 1973.

Furthermore, asbestos remains in older buildings, particularly homes, factories, schools, and commercial buildings.

Likewise, older products containing asbestos, including common household items such as toasters and hair dryers, remain in use. Americans will continue to be impacted by the toxic mineral for many years to come.

Q: OTHER THAN MESOTHELIOMA, WHAT DISEASES ARE CAUSED BY ASBESTOS?

Despite the decline in asbestos use in the United States, the portion of the population suffering from asbestos-related disease continues to increase. Due to the long latency period of the asbestos-related diseases, new cases are still rapidly being diagnosed. Epidemiological studies indicate that we are just hitting the peak of new cases of asbestos-related diseases being diagnosed.

Since asbestosis guidelines were issued in 1979, approximately 45,000 Americans have died from asbestos-related disease. Individuals exposed to asbestos are at greater risk for asbestosis, pleural abnormalities, mesothelioma, and other forms of cancer.

Asbestosis is a chronic lung disease that arises when asbestosis fibers scar of lung tissue. This scarring leads to the thickening and hardening of lung tissues, as well as breathing complications. Symptoms of asbestosis include labored breathing during routine tasks and exercise, chest pain, and coughing. As is the case with mesothelioma, symptoms of asbestosis may take many years to appear. While incurable, asbestosis is treatable, and people can live decades with the disease. However, asbestosis increases the risk of developing lung cancer and heart failure.

Asbestos exposure has been linked to a variety of cancers, including cancers of the lung, bladder, breast, colon, pancreas, and prostate. Moreover, smoking greatly increases the risk of developing asbestos-related disease, particularly lung cancer.

Q: WHO IS AT RISK OF EXPOSURE TO ASBESTOS?

Asbestos is so commonly present throughout the U.S. that most people have been around it at some point but at levels too low to cause disease. It is commonly encountered in everyday items and materials, such as insulation in walls and attics, vinyl tiles, shingles, house siding, blankets protecting water pipes, and car brakes. However, asbestos is hazardous only when encountered in sufficient concentrations.

The majority of asbestos-related disease cases occur in individuals who were exposed to asbestos in their workplaces. Family members of these workers are at risk when an at-risk workers brings home asbestos on their clothing and equipment.

Hundreds of occupational workers are affected by asbestos exposure. Military veterans are also at significant risk, particularly U.S. Navy veterans who served during World War II and the Korean War. These veterans have the single highest incidence of asbestos-related disease. Among everyday occupations, plumbers, pipefitters, steam fitters, and electricians are among the most vulnerable to asbestos-related disease. In addition, asbestos is a potential hazard to anyone working in shipbuilding, commercial product manufacturing, power plants, construction, automotive and aircraft mechanics, metal working, tool making, firefighting, and oil refining.

Other potentially hazardous sources of asbestos include homes and apartments built before 1980 and asbestos mines or other natural asbestos deposits, particularly parts of California and Montana.

Q: WHAT SHOULD I DO IF I SUSPECT THERE IS ASBESTOS IN MY HOME?

If the building materials in your home are not damaged, they should be left alone. They generally won't pose a health risk. Without a label indicating asbestos, you usually cannot tell if a material contains asbestos just by looking at it. But disturbing asbestos-containing materials risks setting loose otherwise contained asbestos fibers.

If you are planning to remodel your home or if your home has damaged building materials, you should have it inspected by a trained and accredited asbestos professional. The professional should take samples for analysis. Do not attempt to take samples yourself.

If you suspect a material or object contains asbestos in your home, take every precaution to avoid damaging it. You may limit activities in the vicinity of the materials to prevent disturbing the asbestos and releasing fibers.

Q: WHAT SHOULD I DO IF I SEE LOOSE ASBESTOS?

If you suspect debris contains loose asbestos, retain a trained and accredited asbestos professional to repair or remove the asbestos. Do not dust, sweep, or vacuum asbestos-containing debris unless it is impossible to prevent access or traffic through them.

If it is absolutely impossible to prevent people from encountering and potentially disturbing loose asbestos, have it cleaned with a wet mop using a mask to prevent asbestos inhalation. Be sure everyone accessing the area uses respiratory protection, such as a mask.

Q: HOW DO I IDENTIFY AND RETAIN AN ASBESTOS PROFESSIONAL?

The EPA maintains a list of agencies for each state which regulate handling asbestos (https://www.epa.gov/asbestos/state-asbestos-contacts). In turn, these agencies maintain a list of licensed and accredited professionals in your area.

To avoid conflicts of interest, you should hire one professional to inspect and assess your asbestos needs and a separate, unrelated professional to do the actual repair/removal.

Any professional you retain should be able to provide evidence of their accreditation. Ask your asbestos professionals to document their completion of federal or state-approved training, as well as references and a list of similar projects they have recently completed.

You can also check on the past performance of your asbestos professionals with your local air pollution control board, the local agency responsible for worker safety, and the Better Business Bureau. You should ask whether the firm has any safety violations and whether it has any legal actions filed against it.

When you find and retain your professional, make sure the inspection will include a complete visual examination, careful collection, and laboratory analysis of samples. If asbestos is found, the professional should provide a written evaluation describing its location, the extent of damage to it, and recommendations for correction or prevention.

According to the EPA, your contractor should follow the following procedures to prevent or minimize hazard to you:

- Avoid spreading or tracking asbestos dust into other areas of your home;
- Dispose of all materials, disposable equipment and clothing used in the job in sealed, leak-proof, and labeled heavy-duty plastic bags;
- Only use a HEPA vacuum, never a non-HEPA vacuum;
- Do not break removed material into small pieces;
- Apply a wetting agent to the asbestos material with a hand sprayer that creates a fine mist before removal, because wet fibers do not float in the air as easily as dry fibers and will be easier to clean up;
- Seal the work area from the rest of the house using plastic sheeting and duct tape, and turn off the heating and air conditioning system. For some repairs, such as pipe insulation removal, plastic glove bags may be adequate. They must be sealed with tape and properly disposed of when the job is complete;
- Ensure the work site is clearly marked as a hazard area. Do not allow household members and pets into the area until work is completed; and
- Ensure that the worksite is visually free of dust and debris.

Obtain written assurance that all procedures have been followed when the job is complete. You should also obtain a disposal manifest to verify that the material will be disposed of in a landfill licensed to receive asbestos.

Once the work is completed, clean the entire area thoroughly with wet mops, wet rags, sponges, or HEPA vacuum cleaners. Never use regular vacuum cleaners for this.

Once any asbestos removal work is completed, the inspection professional who performed the initial analysis should return and take a post-work air quality sample after the work is complete to ensure that asbestos levels in the area have not increased in the process.

For brake and clutch repairs, use only repair shops following Occupational Safety and Health Administration (OSHA) regulations.

JOSEPH SHANNON

I am first and foremost a husband and father. My wife Michelle and I just celebrated our 29th anniversary. Anyone that knows us realizes that Michelle is the MVP of our family and has been responsible for the heavy lifting in our household. She has run the Shannon household with grace and class while I represented people at the law practice.

We have been blessed with six children: Emma, Clare, Kate, Will, Nora and Johnny. Their ages range from 24 to 10. Our lives revolve around our family. Michelle has made it clear that we are all expected to eat dinner together every night if we are able.

I have thoroughly enjoyed coaching every one of my children in some form of sport from soccer to cross country to basketball, mainly at St. Joan of Arc Catholic School in Lisle, Illinois. Our lives revolve around our parish and community. Despite the siren call for non-stop working at the law practice, I have found that none of these activities have adversely affected my professional life.

My parents, Tom and JoAnne Shannon, had ten children in Yakima, Washington. I am number nine. My parents made sure we all received a great education at St. Paul's grade school and Carroll High School. I am extremely grateful to my parents and to my siblings Tom, Mary Jo, Pat, Kathleen, John, Maureen, Anne, and Terry. All of them taught me what it is like to be a good person. I am especially grateful to my mother and father who constantly prayed for me and encouraged me throughout their lifetime, even though I was a very selfish and vain person. My mother and father always reminded me that everything I am and everything I have is a gift from God. I profoundly believe that through my mother's saintly devotion and prayers, I have been blessed beyond my wildest dreams. My father has been a constant conscience for me. I seek the advice of my 98-year-old father now more than I ever have.

I was very fortunate to attend the University of Portland and University of Notre Dame Law School. The best part of Notre Dame is that I met Michelle there, and we were married two years later. I have practiced law in Illinois, Oregon, and Washington states, as well as admitted to practice in other states for cases throughout the years.

The professional success I have enjoyed is derived from many factors. I have had tremendous support from my wife Michelle in allowing me to venture off the big law firm path and begin a practice representing people in 1996. For her leap of faith when we had two little girls under the age of two, I am eternally grateful. I am also grateful to my in-laws Tony and Carmella Aceto and to Danielle and Tom, Nicole and Greg, and Anthony for all their support over the years. I am also thankful to my legal mentors Tom Tongue and Jeff Singer. I would like to thank all my clients who have allowed me to represent them over the years. Although I serve them, I learn from working with them through their difficult circumstances. It has brought me a better level of understanding of the importance of family.

I am grateful to work with a terrific team here at Shannon Law Group, P.C. They are all MVPs in my book.

My ancestors immigrated to this great country in the hopes of a better life for their family. To my grandparents, John and Anna, Joseph and Anne, and all of their ancestors and descendants, I know for certain that I drink from the wells that were dug deep by my terrific family before me.

In summary, I didn't hit a triple. I was born on third base.

SIGN UP FOR OUR FREE NEWSLETTER

Shannon Law Group, P.C., publishes a monthly newsletter with updates on our firm, as well as important notices on the legal landscape affecting the rights of you and your family. It addresses both national and Illinois issues.

If you wish to receive our free newsletter, fill in this form and send it to us:

Mail: **Shannon Law Group, P.C.**
135 South LaSalle Street, Suite 2200
Chicago, Illinois 60603

Email: **Joseph@shannonlawgroup.com**

Name: _____

Address: _____

City: _____

State: _____ Zip: _____

Email: _____

Shannon Law Group

A Professional Corporation

Chicago | Woodridge

135 South LaSalle Street, Suite 2200
Chicago, Illinois 60603

3550 Hobson Road, Suite 403
Woodridge, Illinois 60517
www.shannonlawgroup.com
Tel. 312.578.9501
Fax. 312.268.5474
Email: joseph@shannonlawgroup.com

WA